D0294578

LAWSON LIBRARY
R36537L0121

FOOD FOR LIFE

by John Baines

SUSTAINABLE FUTURES

Evans

WWF

Published by Evans Brothers Limited
2A Portman Mansions
Chiltern Street,
London W1U 6NR

Produced for Evans Brothers Limited by
White-Thomson Publishing Ltd
210 High Street,
Lewes, East Sussex
BN7 2NH

Editorial: Catherine Clarke
Design: Tinstar Design Ltd (www.tinstar.co.uk)
Consultant: Kate Bowie
WWF reviewers: Patricia Kendell and Cherry Duggan
Picture research: Amy Sparks

Printed in China by WKT on chlorine-free
paper from sustainably managed forests.

British Library Cataloguing in Publication Data.

Baines, John D
Food for life. - (Sustainable futures)
1. Food supply - Juvenile literature
2. Food industry and trade - Juvenile literature
3. Agriculture - Juvenile literature
4. Sustainable development - Juvenile literature
I. Title
338.1'9

ISBN-13: 9780237527617
ISBN-10: 0237527618

WWF and the Sustainable Futures series

There are many environmental problems facing our planet, but there is much that we can all do to improve the situation.

WWF works to save endangered species, protect endangered spaces and address global threats to nature such as climate change. That is why we are happy to be associated with the "Sustainable Futures" series, which offers information for you to learn from, think about and act on. Your actions will be crucial to the future of planet Earth.

For further information, please contact:

WWF-UK
Panda House, Weyside Park
Godalming, Surrey GU7 1XR
Telephone: 01483 426444
Fax: 01483 426409
http://www.wwf.org.uk

Acknowledgements

The publishers would like to thank the following for permission to reproduce photographs: Corbis pp. 9 (Richard Bickel), 11 (Paul A. Souders), 15 (Liba Taylor), 17 (Macduff Everton), 20 (Hans Georg Roth), 28 (Gideon Mendel), 30 (Jim Richardson), 32 (Adrian Arbib), 43 (Gary Braasch); Photolibrary pp. 16 (Digitalvision), 19 (OSF), 21, (Index Stock Imagery), 29 (Index Stock Imagery), 38 (Plainpicture), 39 (Pacific Stock), 41 (OSF); Photolibrary.com (Australia) p. 42; Topfoto (National Pictures) p. 44; p. 31 courtesy of Unilever; WTPix pp. 4, 5, 6, 7, 8, 13, 14, 18, 22, 23, 24, 25, 26, 27, 34, 35, 37, 40.

Cover photograph reproduced with permission of OSF/Photolibrary/Jon Arnold Images.

Contents

CHAPTER 1

The importance of food and farming

The population of the world is growing and is now over 6 billion. Farming has successfully increased food production, but some of the methods used are not sustainable. Sustainability in farming means:

- the ability to produce enough food to feed everyone now and in the future
- producing a good quality, high yielding crop
- using as few chemicals and fertilisers as possible
- conserving local plants and animals
- supporting thriving farming communities.

Eat to live

Humans need fuel to live. Food is our fuel and our bodies work best if they are topped up with a mix of different types of food. Humans can eat fruit, vegetables, meat, fish, dairy products, eggs, grains such as wheat and rice, seeds and nuts. This is a more varied diet than most other animals. Humans are omnivores. This has helped us to survive in many different environments from hot humid forests, through to deserts and temperate lands and right into the freezing cold lands of the Arctic. Only Antarctica has no permanent habitations.

Fresh fruit, such as these apples from an orchard in Canada, is an important part of a healthy diet. Using modern farming methods an apple might be sprayed 16 times with 36 different chemicals.

Drought in Tanzania caused this maize crop to fail. Maize provides food for this woman's family and a cash crop to sell. What will the family do now?

The start of the food chain

Food provides the energy the body needs to grow, keep warm, stay active and think. All food originates from plants. Green plants are the only organisms in the natural world that can manufacture their own food. Through a process called photosynthesis, plants are able to convert the energy from the Sun into food. Animals eat plants or other animals that have eaten plants – some animals eat both.

A balanced diet

If our bodies do not have enough of the right types of food then they will not work properly because they will be malnourished. We can become ill and in extreme cases we can die. We need water as well as food. Our bodies can manage without food for several days without too much harm, but we need water much more frequently.

Photosynthesis

Photosynthesis is the first step in the food chain that connects all living things. Photosynthesis begins when light strikes a plant's leaves. Cells in the plant's leaves contain chlorophyll, which interacts with sunlight to split the water in the plant into its basic components. Carbon dioxide enters the leaf and combines with the stored energy in the cells to produce a simple sugar that becomes the food for the plant. Plants store the food in stems, roots, seeds or fruit. Animals such as humans can obtain this energy directly by eating the plant, its seeds or its fruit.

Rice is the staple food for one third of the Earth's population. In the tropics it is grown in paddy fields like these in southern India.

The origins of farming

For most of our 3 million-year history humans have collected food from the wild by gathering plants and fruits and eating some meat after a successful hunt. About 8000 to 10,000 years ago there was an agricultural revolution. Seeds from plants that humans ate most often were planted in cleared ground close to where they lived. With the plants in one place, the people had more control over their food supply and did not have to travel around to find food.

Around this time, humans began to keep and breed animals. Animals provided food and many other useful products. Their skins could be used for shelter or clothing, their bones for needles or digging the ground.

All our domestic animals have their origins in wild animals, but over the centuries many of their wild characteristics have been bred out. Farming has largely replaced hunting and gathering as our means of providing food. Larger permanent settlements developed because people no longer had to move around in search of food.

Population growth and food supply

The fastest growth of the human population has taken place since the 1700s. Thomas Malthus (1766–1834) noted that population growth was faster than the growth in the food supply. He predicted that if population growth was allowed to continue at the same rate there would be a shortage of food and people would starve to death. His worst predictions did not come true because farmers raised their output. Farmers currently produce enough food to feed more than 6 billion people. However, 800 million people are still malnourished because they cannot afford to buy the food, or the food is not available where they live.

The agricultural revolution has been so successful that farming is able to support a world population of more than 6 billion people. Before farming, the human population was probably less than 10 million.

Plants grown by farmers

There are more than 250,000 species of plants. Humans have used about 5000 of these to supply food, but today only about 150 species are grown commercially. However, most of our food supply depends on only twenty staple crops. The top three are rice, wheat and maize. These supply nearly 60 per cent of the world's calories and protein.

Too few varieties?

Traditionally, farmers bred and grew different varieties of each species to take advantage of local conditions. In 1949, for example, farmers in China were growing about 10,000 varieties of wheat. Today, Chinese farmers are growing only 1000 varieties.

In local markets, such as this one in Thailand, it is often possible to buy local food crops that you might not find in a supermarket.

Food for all

The Food and Agricultural Organisation (FAO) believes there should be enough food for everyone over the next 25 years. This is good news, but many modern farming practices are actually making the Earth as a whole less productive by damaging or destroying its ecosystems, changing the climate and polluting the environment.

Food for the future

As farming expands, there are fewer places for wildlife to live. Tropical rainforests are very rich ecosystems with a huge variety of plant and animal species. They are also home to many native peoples. The forests help control the global climate, local weather, flooding and soil erosion. But these forests are being destroyed at an alarming rate. In Brazil, soya beans are grown and sold to feed farm animals in Europe and China. This soya bean farming has resulted in a 40 per cent increase in the loss of the Amazon forests over the last few years. But who should be held responsible for this deforestation? The people clearing the land to grow soya, or the people who eat the animals the soya is fed to?

Farm chemicals increase yields, but can harm wildlife and people, as well as polluting the environment.

Fossil fuels are used when growing and transporting farm products. The burning of fossil fuels releases carbon dioxide into the atmosphere. Carbon dioxide is recognised by most scientists as one of the major causes of global warming. The effects of global warming will have an impact on farming.

Only a few workers are needed to cultivate the land using modern farming methods and machines. In Canada, only about 3 per cent of the population work in farming.

The challenge

Although farming and food production can have a negative impact, there are benefits, too. Applying scientific knowledge to agriculture has enabled us to treble food production with only a small increase in the area being farmed. If these new developments had not taken place then even larger parts of the world's natural forests, grasslands and recreational areas would have been cleared for farming. The alternative would mean a shortage in food leading to starvation. The big challenge for the future is to find ways of feeding a population that is expected to grow to 12 billion, while protecting people, natural systems and farm animals. In other words we need to create sustainable farming systems.

Cuban farmers were badly affected when financial assistance from the Soviet Union was withdrawn. Ploughs being pulled by cattle became a common sight because farmers were unable to afford fuel, which prevented them using machinery such as tractors.

Case study: Sustainable farming in Cuba

Cuba's farming suffered heavily when the Soviet Union collapsed in the 1990s. The state-controlled farming system had large farms producing export crops. It depended on imported chemicals, seeds, machinery and oil. Financial assistance from the Soviet Union suddenly stopped. The country could no longer afford to import food, fertilisers and other farm chemicals. Starvation loomed. In answer to the crisis, Cuba has combined organic farming with a new system of urban gardening. Former waste areas in towns are now lush plots of vegetables, spices and fruit grown by local people and sold to local people. These small-scale units run by families are now able to feed Cuba without the use of artificial chemicals. The families protect the quality of the soil with compost and by rotating crops. The plots provide food and employment and a small income for the families.

CHAPTER 2

From natural to farmed landscapes

Farming changes the way the world looks and the way people live, sometimes in ways that are not sustainable.

Changing the landscape

All over the world farmers have changed their landscape to make it better for farming. These new landscapes are known as cultural landscapes, but are so familiar to us that we often think of them as the natural landscape.

The Netherlands is a small, low-lying country on the coast of Europe with a population of over 16 million. One third of the country lies below the high tide level. The lowest point is -6.7 metres. To make more space, land has been reclaimed from the sea and lakes. This reclaimed land is called a polder. Water from the polders drains into ditches and from there is pumped up into channels that carry the water to the sea. Large banks called dykes protect the polders from flooding again. Windmills that still dot the landscape were used to drive the pumps that moved the water uphill. Although the windmills are still maintained in working order, electrical pumps do most of the pumping today. Much of the reclaimed area is farmed. Farming includes growing flowers, fruit and vegetables, and rearing cattle, sheep and pigs.

The prairies of North America and the steppes of south-east Europe were once open grasslands on which wild animals such as buffalo used to graze. Much of the area has been ploughed and planted with cereal crops such as wheat and maize. In Western Europe, most of the ancient forests have been lost to a patchwork landscape of fields surrounded by hedges or walls. Elsewhere, deserts have been turned into farmland by building canals to carry water to the land.

Farming changes the landscape. Windmills were used to help drain this area in the Netherlands that was once covered by water. The land here is lower than the level of the sea.

In California the landscape has canals, ditches, water towers and other infrastructure to carry water to areas that would otherwise be too dry to cultivate. The Narmada canal in Gujarat, India, is the world's largest irrigation canal. The main canal is 444 kilometres long, and with 31 branch canals the total length is 3000 kilometres.

Sustainable farming and the landscape

Are these landscapes sustainable? A sustainably farmed landscape is one that does not need high quantities of energy, chemicals and other resources to keep it in good condition. It is most likely to be a landscape of small scale, with mixed farming that recognises that its use is limited by climate and soil conditions.

Case study: A heritage landscape

The Ifugao rice fields (above) cover 20,000 hectares along the Cordillera mountain range on the island of Luzon in the Philippines. The rice paddies were constructed hundreds of years ago and they make a spectacular landscape in the form of terraces. Water is carefully channelled from streams through the fields into the river at the bottom of the valley. The terraces can only be maintained with a lot of human effort because the slopes are too steep for machines. Although a World Heritage site, the terraces are suffering from neglect and environmental degradation as local people find alternative sources of food that do not demand such heavy work.

The Asian vulture is one of many species that has declined due to changes in traditional farming practices. If new, safer drugs are used on cattle by vets it may reverse the situation in India.

All change for wildlife

Without human interference, all areas develop ecosystems that reflect the local conditions. In areas of very low rainfall, there are few plants and animals. In Arctic conditions, plants and animals have to be able to protect themselves from intense cold. Two of the richest ecosystems (ones where a lot of different species live) are tropical rainforests on the land and coral reefs in the sea.

Farming and wildlife

Farmers remove the natural vegetation and replace it with plants they wish to grow. So far, they have converted about 30 per cent of the world's land area to farmland. In eastern Asia it is over 40 per cent. When this happens, there is less space for the wild plants and animals that originally lived there. A new, farmed ecosystem is made and this can attract new plants and animals. Many traditional farming systems managed to co-exist with a variety of wild plants, animals and insects and were sustained over hundreds of years.

Modern farming systems that use a lot of artificial chemicals to control weeds, insects and fungi, or to treat animals, can have a devastating effect on wildlife. For example, Asian vultures in India have declined by 95 per cent over the past 10 years. These birds are important because they feed on the bodies of dead animals that would otherwise spread disease as they rot. Research has shown that the vultures die after eating the carcasses of livestock that have been treated with a common drug used by vets. If a new, safer drug can be found it may be possible to reverse the decline in the vulture population.

Farming and conservation

Many farmers already try to find a balance between making a living from farming and protecting the environment. In Europe, this should become easier in the future. Over the coming years, the European Union will pay farmers to farm in ways that protect the landscape and the wildlife that lives in it. This should help to make farming more sustainable.

Is organic farming sustainable?

Organic farmers use modern methods, but they do not use artificial chemicals. For example, farmers use manure and compost rather than artificial fertilisers. Organic produce is becoming more popular and people choose to buy it for a number of reasons. For example, they consider animals are treated better and are not fed additives, the food is healthier and the farming methods are more sustainable. However, is the produce any better, and are organic methods more sustainable than ordinary farming? There is some disagreement on this issue:

"When I first started farming organically my real aim was to explore the best ways of developing a sustainable system of food production. Organic farming was, and still is, the most effective system of applying what I thought to be the principles of sustainable agriculture."

Prince Charles

"If you stick to the science, organic farms produce lower yields and more pests and there is no evidence to substantiate claims [that the food is healthier for you]."

Professor Michael Wilson, chief executive of the UK Horticultural Research Unit

Modern commercial farming like this strawberry field in Egypt, leaves little space for wildlife. Chemicals sprayed on to the fruits also reduce the number of insects that are eaten by birds and other animals.

Changing lives

Farming has changed the way people live their lives. Those who planted crops (arable farmers) became more settled as they needed to tend their fields regularly. Farmers produced more food than they needed for themselves and were able to exchange this food for other goods and services. Communities with a range of farming and non-farming activities developed. The ancient civilisations of the Middle East with their villages and cities were based on farming.

Pastoralists are farmers who move with their animals to find the best grazing land. There has been conflict between pastoralists and arable farmers because arable farming reduces the amount of land for grazing and often it is the best grazing land that is used. To reduce this conflict in Mali, a Pastoral Code has been agreed that allows the pastoralists access to grazing lands, including the fields of the arable farmers after the harvest. The farmers benefit from this because the dung from the cattle fertilises the soil.

In parts of India there has been a relationship between arable farmers and pastoralists for centuries. The dung from the cattle provides fuel, fertiliser and building material for the farmers. The pastoralists are able to graze their cattle on the farmland and use facilities such as medical and veterinary care in the villages.

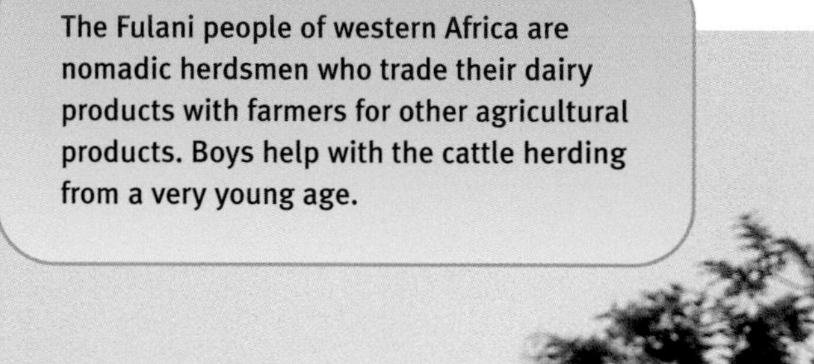

The Fulani people of western Africa are nomadic herdsmen who trade their dairy products with farmers for other agricultural products. Boys help with the cattle herding from a very young age.

Rural or urban?

Throughout all of human history, more people have lived in rural areas than urban areas because providing food was essential and needed a large workforce. More and more tools and machines have been invented to help farmers produce food with a smaller workforce. Today, the number of farmers needed to feed the world's population is at its lowest. Within the decade 2000 to 2010, the number of people living in towns will be more than 50 per cent for the first time. We will be a planet of city-dwellers rather than country-dwellers.

Quality of life

Farmers and their communities respond to the environments in which they live. Many different farming and social systems have evolved around the world as a result. These rural communities continue to evolve today. To be sustainable, the communities in which people live should provide a decent quality of life. That means the people should be able to make a good living, have decent shelter, clean water, and sanitation. They should feel secure and be able to make use of services such as health and education. Many people living in rural communities worldwide do not have a good quality of life.

More people are becoming city-dwellers, but many have to live in shanty towns like this one in Kariobangi, Kenya, Africa, because they are too poor to afford a proper home or a decent quality of life. Buying food takes much of their income.

Unsustainable farming from the past

History has many disaster stories caused by unsustainable farming. The Mayans of Central America (2500 BC to AD 900) developed very intensive farming systems with fields created on steep slopes and areas of drained swamp. Eventually, the natural systems could not cope. Soil erosion and high levels of silt in the rivers damaged the fields, and food production declined substantially.

North Africa provided the Romans with grain but, as more of the natural vegetation was removed to make way for crops, soil erosion began to damage the whole area. Much of it remains as desert to this day.

CHAPTER 3

Farming in the developed world

Modern farming methods enable one farmer to produce enough food to feed thousands of people and to use land that would otherwise be unsuitable for farming. People in the developed world have more than enough food available to them, and are able to buy a greater variety of foods than ever before. The food is relatively cheap to buy and because of fast transport from grower to market, most can be bought out of season. But all of these benefits come at a cost, and modern farming is criticised for not being sustainable.

Modern farming methods

Modern farming is productive because farmers have been encouraged with financial grants from their governments to increase food production. A huge and profitable farming industry has grown to supply the demand for food.

Arable farming

In arable farming, machinery enables one person to farm large areas of land. A farmer has a huge number of chemicals available to control weeds, insects and fungi that would otherwise reduce productivity. Fertilisers are used to make the crops grow better. Land that is too boggy for crops can be drained, and in areas where the rainfall is too low or unreliable for farming, irrigation schemes can provide water for cultivation. Scientists have also developed varieties of plants that have higher yields, are resistant to diseases, and will still do well in less than perfect conditions.

These chickens will spend the rest of their lives in crowded cages laying eggs. They cannot live anything like a natural life. Is this acceptable if it means we can have very cheap eggs?

Animal farming

Animal farming has also become more intensive so that more meat, eggs and dairy products are available at low cost. Whereas 100 years ago good dairy cows produced an average of 20 litres of milk a day, they can now produce 50 to 70 litres.

Domesticated animals are the descendants of wild animals, but their lives are now carefully controlled. For example, chicken has become a popular food and 3 billion chickens are slaughtered each year in the USA alone. Most chickens are kept in crowded barns with only a space of about 15 centimetres by 15 centimetres for each animal. Farmers encourage the chickens to eat by artificially making the days longer and the nights shorter. The chickens can be ready for slaughter in as little as 6 weeks.

Other animals farmed intensively include pigs, cattle and fish. While this is very efficient, it raises a moral issue. Is it right to treat animals in this way?

A sustainable approach to animal farming would reduce the intensity of production and promote the long-term welfare of the animals. A more balanced existence may produce less, but energy and other inputs could be reduced as well. The animals would be healthier, so medicine and veterinary bills could be less, too.

Free-range farming is an alternative to battery farming. These pigs are being raised for their meat, but while growing they are free to roam in their field and have shelters where they can go for rest or protection.

Chemicals and the environment

Fertilisers improve plant growth. When it rains, any fertiliser left in the soil can be washed into rivers, streams and ponds, where it fertilises the plants. Algae grow on the surface of water and use up a lot of oxygen. An increase in the amount of algae means that sunlight cannot get to the plants growing in the water and they die. As they decay, they use up even more oxygen. Fish in the water will also die if they do not have enough oxygen. This whole process is known as eutrophication.

Chemicals used to control pests, weeds and fungi can get into the food chain. Pesticide residues on foods we eat might damage our health. Research by the UK government in 2001 showed that 0.7 per cent of the food that is eaten contains pesticide residues above the maximum permitted level. This doesn't sound very much, but these chemicals can build up in the body.

Chemicals are also blamed for a decline in certain species of birds. Herbicides and pesticides control weeds and insects. Birds that feed on the seeds of weeds or on insects, suffer when these are killed off.

Wasting food

If more of the food produced worldwide was eaten rather than thrown away, then food production could become less intensive because not as much would be needed.

For every adult in the UK, more than £480 worth of food is wasted each year. In the USA the food wasted could feed more than 49 million people. A lot of food is thrown away because it has minor imperfections and so is not put on sale. Restaurants, school canteens and other eating-places have to cater for a range of menus and appetites. Up to a third of all the food they buy is thrown away.

In less wealthy countries any waste food is either saved for later, or fed to animals such as hens, pigs or cattle that in turn provide food. Alternatively, if the waste food is not suitable for animals it is composted and used to improve the soil. These are more sustainable ways of dealing with unwanted food.

This urban farmer near Kano, Nigeria, is sorting through waste. Organic material is separated from other waste and used as fertiliser. This contributes to a sustainable way of farming.

Modern commercial farming can encourage wildlife. On this farm in the UK the farmer has left hedges and an uncultivated strip as habitats for wildlife.

Farming methods and the environment

Changing farming practices can also have an impact on wildlife. Removing trees, hedges, ditches and ponds to make larger fields reduces the amount of habitat available to wildlife. Leaving just a few wild areas can provide spaces for wildlife. Joining the wild areas up to form wild corridors is the most beneficial way for wildlife to thrive. Ploughing in the stubble of cereal fields and reseeding them in autumn instead of spring increases the farmer's yield, but reduces the amount of cover and food available for birds.

Larger fields, without trees, hedges or ditches, can be prone to soil erosion. There are no barriers to the wind, and during dry, windy periods soil can be blown away as it was from the 'Dust Bowl' area in the USA in the 1930s. Another problem is declining soil quality caused by low levels of organic materials in the soil. These can be replaced by spreading compost or manure. Erosion can also be caused by water running down slopes. Plants slow down the water flow and hold the soil in place.

Intensive animal farming can also create problems. Mountains of waste pile up and can pollute the land. Disease can spread quickly between animals. In 2001, for example, 6 million animals had to be killed in the UK to try to stop the spread of foot-and-mouth disease.

Modern farming has brought great benefits, but it has also brought some unexpected and unwanted problems. Now that these problems are recognised, many farmers are managing some areas for wildlife.

Changing the rules

Government policies influence patterns of farming. Since the Second World War, most governments have encouraged farmers to increase production with financial incentives, or subsidies. Imports were also restricted. Protection of the environment was not considered.

People can buy locally grown or produced foods direct from farmers at farmers' markets such as this one in Pula, Croatia. Customers can ask the farmers how the food was produced. These markets are an alternative to the supermarket for fresh foods.

Supermarkets and sustainable food

Most people in the developed world do their food shopping in a supermarket. Supermarkets can determine what is available to us to buy and say that price is more important to consumers than anything else. They tell farmers what to produce and how to produce it and push for low prices. Supermarkets are also in a strong position to support sustainable farming if consumers want this. Issues for discussion could include:

- should supermarkets support local farmers or buy from the cheapest suppliers?
- should fresh food with natural imperfections be sold rather than dumped?
- how can the distance travelled by our food before we eat it (food miles) be reduced?
- should supermarkets sell genetically modified foods?
- should supermarkets ensure fair wages and working conditions for workers: from farmer to food supplier?

"Customers expect retailers to stock a wide range of fruit and vegetables all year round – many of these are either not grown in this country or only seasonally."

Retailer

"Local food markets could deliver on all aspects of sustainable development, economic, environmental and social."

Politician

Farm subsidies

Subsidies have helped farmers modernise and increase production dramatically, but they have also encouraged unsustainable farming practices. Subsidies have also had a damaging effect on the livelihoods of farmers in other countries. Overseas farmers are not always able to sell their produce in countries where subsidies have been given to the local farmers. Is this unfair competition?

In addition, developed countries produce surplus food and this is sold on the world market at very low prices. Rural poverty in Africa is partly caused by this, because farmers there cannot compete with these subsidised low prices. Organisations such as the World Trade Organisation are trying to reduce barriers to free trade.

In Europe, subsidies are being replaced by payments to farmers to farm their land more sustainably. That means being paid for conservation projects, using fewer chemicals on the land, restoring hedges and woodland, or for organic farming. To increase their income, farmers are also diversifying into other activities such as providing camping facilities and bed and breakfast, or using surplus barns for small industrial units.

These measures should help conservation, promote rural employment and make rural areas places where people want to live, work and enjoy life in ways that will allow future generations to do the same.

Meanwhile, the USA is continuing with farm subsidies. In 2002, it was agreed to subsidise US farming with US$190 billion of grants. "This farm bill will put millions of small farmers out of business in Africa," said Mark Ritchie, president of the Institute for Agriculture and Trade Policy in Minneapolis.

Peanut farming in the USA is highly mechanised and subsidised by the government. Subsidised farming prevents fair competition between producers in different countries.

CHAPTER 4

Farming in the developing world

Traditional farming methods can no longer supply enough food for rising populations in developing countries, so agricultural change is necessary. Can food be supplied while protecting the environment and the lives and livelihoods of local people? That is the challenge...

Families of farmers

In developing countries a greater proportion of people live and work in rural areas than in developed countries. In Asia and Africa about 70 per cent of people live in rural areas and are dependent mainly on farming. The populations of developing countries are growing more rapidly than in developed countries, so each year there are more people to feed. Traditional methods of farming cannot supply all the food these people need.

Clean water is essential for health. This new, safe and convenient water supply in an African village will help keep people healthy so they can work on their farmland more effectively.

Case Study: HIV/AIDS and farming in Africa

It is estimated that over half of the 28 million people living with HIV/AIDS in sub-Saharan Africa live in rural areas. Stricken families struggle to produce enough food to survive. Children have to do the work of adults and miss their schooling. In rural areas, food production is declining and farming families are finding it difficult to feed themselves and also have a surplus for sale. Lack of income makes the family even poorer. Without proper health care and affordable drugs, life expectancy is falling. In some areas it is as low as 30 years. HIV/AIDS is a real threat to being able to develop sustainable farming communities in Africa.

The 'Green Revolution'

The 'Green Revolution' of the 1960s and 1970s helped countries such as India to feed their growing populations. It depended on three changes:

- Land not previously farmed was brought into cultivation.
- Two crops a year were planted instead of one. This made it necessary to plant in the dry season, so irrigation schemes were built to supply water.
- New varieties of seeds were used. These give higher yields than traditional ones.

The plan succeeded and between 1961 and 2000 rice and wheat production tripled in the developing countries of Asia.

Most farming families in developing countries are poor, and now they have to contend with an accelerating new problem. Global warming, partly caused by developed countries using large amounts of fossil fuels, is causing the sea level to rise.

Much of the farmland in Bangladesh is low-lying. During this century Bangladesh is likely to lose about 16 per cent of its farmland, causing huge problems for the 17 million farmers who depend on this land for survival. This is an example of how enjoying a high standard of life in one country can make farming unsustainable in another.

In India, 70 per cent of people live in rural areas and make their living from farming. This man is planting rice. Thanks to the improved seeds and farming methods brought by the Green Revolution, his harvest will be increased dramatically. Food production in India is now keeping up with population growth.

Producing food for sale

There is trade between developed and developing countries in food. Tropical fruits, such as bananas, and vegetables, such as sweet potatoes, are popular in developed countries. Producing fruit and vegetables such as these for export, helps farmers in the developing world to earn money.

Crops such as rice and wheat from the USA are for sale in developing countries. US produce is sometimes cheaper than locally produced food, partly due to the US government subsidies to growers. This undermines attempts to help local farmers produce food for local people.

Fair trade

Small-scale farmers in the developing world have to contend with prices that go up and down. If prices remain low they can get into terrible debt and lose everything. Development agencies recognised this problem and started buying direct from farmers at higher prices and marketing the produce through their own shops and catalogues. They called this fair trade.

The first 'Fairtrade Label' was launched in 1986 on coffee from Mexico. Today, there are nineteen organisations, including the 'Fairtrade Foundation', that follow the standards set by Fairtrade Labelling Organisations International. Producers registered with FLO receive a minimum price that covers the cost of production and an extra amount that is invested in the local community. It is now possible to buy a range of fair trade products: many of them alongside other produce on supermarket shelves. The fair trade approach gives farming families a chance to have a sustainable business.

Fair trade organisations such as 'Cafédirect' pay farmers 100 per cent or more above the world market price for the coffee beans inside the berries. Giving the farmer a fair price costs the consumer drinking the coffee very little extra.

Many tropical and subtropical crops such as this tea in Kenya are grown on large plantations. They are usually run by large businesses because small farmers do not have the money needed to develop the land.

Cash crops

Some commodities such as palm oil, soya and tea are often grown on large plantations owned by big companies rather than by individual farmers. Conditions for the workers can be very poor. In west Africa it was found that young children were being recruited to work on cocoa plantations and then being treated as slaves.

For some commodities such as coffee, small farmers use part of their land for growing coffee bushes and set up co-operatives to help them process and sell the beans to agents. Co-operatives can work well for small farmers, but the prices paid for coffee beans are very low because there is a surplus of coffee. A farmer in Guatemala might receive US$1 for a kilogram of beans that sell in the USA for US$18 a kilogram. Such prices do not allow the farming families to pay for their basic needs and are therefore unsustainable.

Food for farm animals

The demand for meat in developed countries has grown so much that a lot of the food needed to feed the animals is imported from the developing world. In Thailand, an area about the size of Ireland (70,000 square kilometres) is used to supply manioc for European cattle. Brazil has become a major supplier of soya beans for European animal feed, but to do this it has cut down a quarter of its Cerrada plateau forest, some 48,560 square kilometres, causing great damage. Back in Europe, safely disposing of the waste from these soya-fed animals is also a problem.

Food miles

Most forms of transportation, especially air travel, require the burning of fossil fuels. The fuel needed to transport food around the world can therefore contribute significantly to global warming.

Urban farming

Cities in developing countries are growing faster than those in developed countries. People moving from rural areas in the hope of finding a better life make up about half of this growth. Many of them remain poor and find it difficult to afford basic necessities such as food, clean water and shelter. Their quality of life is very poor.

Urban farming facts

- In Shanghai, China, 85 per cent of vegetables eaten in the city are grown in the city.
- Urban farming supplies food to 700 million people.
- In Kenya, 17 per cent of urban households keep livestock.
- The campus of Beijing University, China, includes several irrigated rice fields.

Urban agriculture at Kofar Ruwa in the old city of Kano. Urban agriculture plays an important role in urban livelihoods and helps feed the city of Kano.

Case study: China's urban farming

Urban farming is very intensive. In Guangzhou in southern China, a single field can produce up to nine crops a year. The fertility of the soil must be continually renewed. This is done through recycling waste. Recycled human waste, in particular, has long been used in urban agriculture. The waste is collected from households and taken to a cesspool. Once it is rid of pathogens (things that can cause disease), it is applied to the fields. This is becoming less common, however, as farmers choose to use chemical fertilisers instead. There is then the problem of how to dispose of the human waste. In other words, farming is becoming less sustainable.

Supplying food to the cities becomes more expensive when land close to the city is built on. Increasing quantities of food have to be brought greater distances. Roads in developing countries are often poor and congestion in cities means journey times are long. It is common for between 10 and 30 per cent of the produce to spoil during transit. Poor people do not have refrigerators and need to buy fresh food every day. A more sustainable food solution is to support urban farming. This is a system that makes use of small plots of empty land, gardens and even roof tops to grow food and keep animals such as chickens.

In India, dairy cattle are kept in urban areas to supply fresh milk. They can often be seen walking down the street eating waste food from market stalls and houses. Urban farming also helps deal with increasing amounts of urban waste by using organic waste as compost, and waste water for irrigation. Transport time and costs are reduced and the food is fresher and more affordable. Green areas also improve the air quality, help prevent flooding during storms, relieve high summer temperatures and provide quieter areas. Urban farming already makes a contribution to sustainable city living, but city authorities often discourage it.

> *"[When urban farming is] officially sanctioned and promoted, urban agriculture could become an important component of urban development and make more food available to the urban poor [...] urban agriculture can also provide fresher and cheaper produce, more green space, the clearing of garbage dumps and recycling of household waste."*
>
> World Commission on Environment and Development

Herds of cows are kept in Indian cities. Grazing on rubbish is rarely healthy for the cows and they are often in a poor condition.

CHAPTER 5

Globalisation of food and farming

Globalisation is the term used to describe the coming together of countries to work to a common set of rules: rather like trying to make schools have the same school rules wherever they are. For farmers, there are advantages and disadvantages of globalisation.

International action

Defeating hunger is a necessary first step in any sustainable food development programme. In 1996, countries at the 'Food Summit' agreed that by the year 2015 the number of people suffering from malnutrition would be reduced by half.

There are also international aid agencies such as the Red Cross and the Red Crescent that organise food and other aid programmes especially during natural catastrophes, such as drought and flooding, and in areas badly affected by war.

World Trade Organisation (WTO)

The WTO is one of the main promoters of globalisation in food products, and one of the most controversial. It aims to remove all tariffs and subsidies that hinder trade in food and food products. While that may seem fair, it is criticised for not allowing sufficiently for different environmental and social needs around the world. For example, in March 2004 the Indian government refused to increase the subsidy paid to Indian farmers for rice and wheat. This decision will make it easier for US farmers to sell their wheat and rice in India.

This farmer in Haiti is part of a local co-operative that helps peasant coffee farmers process and market their coffee beans. His beans are sold to a fair trade buyer, which means he can earn a good living from his farm.

EU countries will not import beef from the USA if growth hormones have been fed to the cattle. The USA says this is illegal and has reported the matter to the World Trade Organisation. The WTO agree that this is illegal, but the EU will not import the meat because it cannot guarantee there are no health implications.

In turn, this is likely to reduce rural employment in India and further increase poverty. At the same time, the USA subsidises its own farmers and surplus food is sold at very low prices on the world market, undercutting local producers. The Indian government originally refused to increase subsidies to their own farmers so that the USA would consider allowing India to supply more goods and services to them.

Endangered species

In the USA, the Endangered Species Act banned the sale of shrimps caught in nets that endangered turtles. There were complaints from several Asian countries, such as the Philippines, and these complaints were upheld by the WTO. This has meant a continuing threat to the turtle population. Rulings such as these undermine sustainable development.

The World Bank

The World Bank is a major lender of funds for agriculture and other projects in developing countries. The Bank recognises the importance of agriculture to the livelihoods of rural people, but will only fund schemes that are environmentally sustainable and promote sustainable rural communities. In El Salvador, for example, the Bank has supported coffee growing that is less environmentally damaging than normal methods. The environment is benefiting and the local people are earning a good living.

The role of big companies

Farmers have normally bought their seed from one company, fertiliser from another, machinery from another, animal feed from another and so on. When it was time to sell their produce farmers sold at the local market: through a co-operative, direct to a shop or even to the government. This system is now rare, because of the growth of very large agri-businesses that manage the whole process from seed to supermarket shelf. Farmers sell their produce back to the same company that supplied them with seeds. The farmers these companies work with might be in a different country from where the seed is produced and the food is finally eaten.

Consumer questions

Agri-businesses have a lot of control over what we eat and how our food is produced, but they can only sell food that consumers are willing to buy. People are becoming more and more concerned about the safety of their food and the way in which it is produced. Questions they are asking include:

- does it contain any harmful chemical residues?
- is it produced locally?
- have animals been kept humanely?
- is the food GM (Genetically Modified)?

Although genetically modified seeds have been accepted in some countries, such as the USA, there is a lot of resistance to them in most European countries. This worker is extracting corn embryos for the development of a genetically modified crop.

Company responses

Food producers and suppliers have responded by making more information available to customers, and selling things such as free-range eggs, fair trade goods and organic foods as well as refusing to stock produce containing GM foods. These products come from farming systems that are generally more sustainable than conventional ones.

Large multinational companies have a lot of influence over farming, but it is consumers who buy their produce. If consumers demand sustainable agriculture, then it will happen.

Unilever assists Brazilian farmers to grow tomatoes sustainably by helping them to install drip irrigation systems which use less water than standard irrigation systems.

Case study: Unilever and sustainable food

Unilever is one of the world's major producers of food products with interests in 150 developed and developing countries. It is working towards making its farming activities more sustainable.

Unilever's chairman said, "We know we have no choice but to pursue responsible agricultural practices and that this is vital to sustaining a healthy environment and maintaining our reputation as a good corporate citizen."

Unilever set up the Sustainable Agriculture Initiative programme with the help of farmers, scientific advisers and other interested groups. It is aiming to make production of its main crops (palm oil, peas, spinach, tea and tomatoes) sustainable. In Brazil for example, the company is helping farmers to install drip irrigation to tomato growing. Using tubes to deliver small quantities of water and nutrients straight to the plants' roots reduces water use by up to 30 per cent and chemical use by 25 per cent.

Greenpeace is one of the environmental organisations campaigning against GM crops. In the UK, members of Greenpeace have ripped GM crops up to try to stop them from being grown. Tests have shown that GM crops are less good for the environment than conventional ones.

Is globalisation compatible with sustainable farming?

The globalisation of farming seems to favour modern agricultural techniques that are designed to maximise output and profit, with only secondary concern for protecting wildlife, natural resources and rural communities. On the other hand, globalisation is allowing farmers in developing countries to grow high value produce and sell it in developed countries. This in turn enables them to enjoy a higher standard of living. If a large multinational company such as Unilever promotes sustainable development, then it has a huge beneficial impact. Conventional farming also allows the Earth to produce enough food for 6 billion people. The criticism is that it is not sustainable in the long term.

Genetically modified crops

Genetically modified crops are modified with genes from other plants to give them different characteristics. For example, crops can be modified so that they are more productive, withstand drought, have a longer shelf life, are resistant to a certain type of weed killer, or resistant to particular pests. Research published in 2003 showed that the different farming methods associated with most of the GM crops that were tested led to a decline in local wildlife.

Some people and organisations are also suspicious of the motives of the big multinational companies. The new seeds are patented and often require farmers to use the company's own chemicals if the crops are to grow successfully. The world could become dependent on even fewer varieties of crops than it already is. Local varieties of farm plants that have evolved over centuries to suit particular local conditions could also be lost. A few private companies could potentially dominate food supply.

Finding a balance

With an increasing demand for high quality, low cost food products it is necessary to find a balance between commercial food production, managing the rural environment, and maintaining vibrant rural communities. We need to find ways of producing enough food to feed today's expanding population. At the same time, we need to choose sustainable methods of producing and delivering this food that will not deplete vital resources needed to feed future generations.

Sustainable farming

There are no easy or right and wrong answers when deciding what is and what is not sustainable farming, but the following table compares some common opinions about the characteristics of conventional farming and sustainable farming. Most farming practices will have characteristics taken from both sides of the table.

Non-sustainable farming	Sustainable farming
Large farm units	Small, family-sized farm units
Highly mechanised	Labour intensive
High energy input per unit of production	Low energy input per unit of production
Rural communities poorly serviced	Rural communities with good services
High capital costs	Low capital costs
Monoculture (single crop)	Several crops grown in rotation
Intensive animal rearing	Humane animal rearing
Uses artificial fertilisers to increase soil fertility	Uses compost and other organic matter to improve soil fertility
Soil low in organic matter	Soil rich in organic matter
Soil prone to erosion	Soil less prone to erosion
Uses artificial chemicals to control weeds and pests	Uses mulches and weeding to control weeds and natural methods to control pests
Produce travels long distances for sale	Produce sold locally
Biodiversity (variety of life) reduced by farming methods	Biodiversity encouraged by farming methods

CHAPTER 6

Fishing for food

Fish are a very nutritious food and many communities around the world make their living from fishing. Pollution of the oceans and modern fishing methods are threatening fish stocks. Countries are trying to find a better balance between fishing and conservation.

Food from the sea

Oceans cover about 70 per cent of the Earth's surface. Areas such as the Dogger Bank in the North Sea or Grand Banks in the North Atlantic, where fish thrive, are known as fisheries. According to the UN Food and Agricultural Organisation, around 130 million tonnes of fish are caught every year.

Overfishing

It was once thought impossible to overfish the oceans because they are so vast. However, so many fishing fleets from North America and Europe were fishing the Grand Banks that stocks of the popular species of fish started to collapse in the 1960s. Communities along the North Atlantic coast who had made a good living from fishing no longer had a livelihood. Unsustainable fishing had depleted the fish stocks and caused a crisis for the fishing communities.

Scientists are able to estimate what is a sustainable catch, but persuading governments and fishing fleets to accept quotas is more difficult. Fisheries in the North Sea are under threat, but the advice of the scientists to close areas off to fishing is not being taken.

Fish is a very nutritious food. Overfishing in the oceans has reduced stocks so that fish is now very expensive to buy.

Case study: Sustainable fishing in Iceland

Iceland has little good agricultural land, but the North Atlantic waters are very rich in fish. Traditionally, Icelanders have depended on fishing for their food supply and their exports. However, the country was only able to control fishing within 3 miles of its coast. Beyond that, other countries, particularly the UK and Germany, were also fishing and depleting the fish stocks. In 1961, Iceland extended its control to 12 miles, then 50 miles and finally 200 miles. This set off what became known as the 'Cod Wars' because Iceland was determined to protect the fish stocks, and other countries were determined to fish them. Today, all countries have 200-mile Economic Exclusion Zones within which they can control economic development. Iceland limits the fishing around its coasts so that the fisheries can support its people now and in the future.

Fishing techniques

Some fishing techniques pay little attention to protecting the environment or other species that live off the sea. Tuna fishing can be particularly bad for dolphins as tuna swim underneath dolphins. Hundreds of dolphins drown when they become trapped in nets and cannot get to the surface to breathe.

Long-line fishing in the South Atlantic is killing large numbers of albatrosses. The baited lines from the fishing boats attract the birds as they try to get the bait. They get caught up in the line, or get hooked and are dragged under the sea and drown.

Bottom trawling is another damaging practice. Heavy nets up to 400 metres wide are dragged across the ocean floor collecting fish and other marine animals and destroying the seabed. It can take centuries for this habitat to recover. It is rather like destroying a whole forest to catch and eat just a few of the animals that live there.

Fishing communities have accepted that fishing must be sustainable. The holes in nets have been made larger so smaller fish can escape. They have accepted quotas for different species of fish and have limited the number of days they spend at sea.

Many coastal villages make a living from selling fish. These fish on a beach in India are being dried to preserve them because most people do not have refrigerators.

Fish farming

Fisheries are not able to supply enough fish to meet the growing demand, so fish farming (aquaculture) is becoming more common, especially for the more expensive types of fish such as salmon and trout. About 25 per cent of the fish eaten in the world comes from fish farms.

Sustainable fish farming

Fish farming has been practised for centuries as part of a sustainable farming system. In China, for example, a fish farming system operating for more than 1200 years has recently been granted world agricultural heritage status. Young fish are thrown into paddy fields when they are flooded during February. The fish waste and the carbon dioxide they exhale provide nutrients for the growing rice plants. Other plants in the field provide shade, and potential pests provide a supply of food for the fish. The paddy field produces fish and rice, but requires very few extra chemicals. It is an example of sustainable fish farming.

Shrimp farming

Shrimp, or prawns as they are also known, breed in coastal mangrove forests. They have been farmed for centuries and farmers protect the mangroves where they breed. With a growing demand for shrimps in developed countries, entrepreneurs saw an opportunity for large-scale shrimp farming. Sales of shrimp amount to about US$60 billion worldwide. Huge, plastic-lined shrimp ponds have replaced mangrove forests. In these ponds, shrimp are fed on food concentrates containing antibiotics to try and prevent disease. These methods are not sustainable for more than a few years, so once the area is exhausted, a new area of mangrove is destroyed to make way for new farms.

Large-scale commercial shrimp ponds provide jobs, but have replaced mangroves along many coasts in South-East Asia. Mangroves protect the coast from floods and are home to many young fish. These workers are harvesting shrimp from a pond in Songkhia, Thailand.

These 'Chinese fishing nets' are being used at Kochi in India. The nets reach over the water, but are fixed to poles on the land. They are lowered into the water for a few minutes and then lifted out again to see what has been caught. The fishermen using this method of fishing do not need boats.

Pollution from fish farms

Fish farms in developed countries, which produce mainly salmon and trout, are also controversial. Fish farms need sheltered bays and estuaries to avoid damage by storms and large waves. These are the same areas that conservationists and fishing communities want to protect, because they are the breeding grounds for many wild fish. Fish farms create pollution from waste food, waste from the fish and chemicals used to prevent pests and diseases. These damage wild fish and the ecosystems on which they depend.

However, fish farms can also provide much needed employment in isolated rural communities. Production of fish is cheaper than catching wild fish and, as a result, the price to the customer is lower. Many more people are able to afford to buy salmon, which is considered a luxury food.

Finding a balance between expanding the economy, protecting the environment and building healthy communities is not easy.

"The extensive development of aquaculture industries off Java and Sumatra has led to the destruction (approximately 40 per cent since the mid 1980s) of large areas of mangrove forests."

The British Embassy in Jakarta

"It's estimated 600,000 people in Bangladesh are dependent on shrimp farming. Many of them come from poor families like mine with no other source of income. Without this farm we would be totally penniless."

Mr Rahman who runs a 10,000 square metre saltwater shrimp farm near the town of Khulna, Bangladesh. His family help him to rear thousands of shrimp for export to Europe and the USA.

Fish and fish products make up more than 70 per cent of Iceland's export of goods. Fishing is carefully controlled so that it is sustainable and able to support future generations.

Sustainable fishing

Fish are a renewable food resource. For more than a billion people they are invaluable, contributing to their food supply, their livelihood and their health. If fish are so important to so many people, why do we allow more fish to be removed from the sea than nature can replace?

'Law of the Sea'

Most countries with a sea coast are involved in some kind of fishing and they all want access to the best fishing areas, but do not want anyone else fishing in what they consider their own fishing areas. The UN Convention on the Law of the Sea, agreed in 1982, is a means of sharing responsibility for living and non-living marine resources. It agreed that all countries could control economic activity up to 200 miles, and in some cases further, from their coasts. This included many of the most important fisheries and meant that countries could choose to manage their fish stocks sustainably.

EU Common Fisheries Policy

The European Union has a Common Fisheries Policy that is agreed by all EU countries. Although scientists have told governments that fishing must stop completely in some areas if stocks are to survive, governments have failed to implement their recommendations. Although fishing is very much regulated, scientists do not think it is currently sustainable.

Codes of conduct

In 1995 a responsible fishing Code of Conduct was agreed by nations. Although not enforceable, it provides guidelines on sustainable fishing. It is not only the fishing industry that has to make changes. It is also necessary to stop polluting the oceans, destroying coastal habitats in order to build ports, tourist facilities, factories and so on, and to reduce soil erosion so that silt washed off the land does not kill the coral reefs where so many fish begin their lives.

Guidelines for responsible aquaculture, such as the Kyoto Declaration on Aquaculture, are now becoming more common. All of them aim to create a sustainable aquaculture sector that is environmentally responsible.

It takes a long time to move from recognition to solution of a problem, but change is taking place. The Marine Stewardship Council (MSC) certifies fish from well-managed fisheries. It is hoping to encourage consumers to buy only those seafood products that bear their label of approval. Unilever, the world's largest buyer of seafood, and WWF, the international conservation organisation, set up the MSC in 1997.

Whale hunting or watching?

Whales are mammals that live in the sea. Whales were hunted because they provided many valuable resources, from food to lubricant oils. By the middle of the last century many of the larger species had been hunted to near extinction. A ban on hunting was agreed in 1982. In 2005, Japan, Norway and Iceland were arguing that some commercial hunting should start again as stocks were recovering. However, most other countries want a complete ban on whale hunting: mainly because it is considered unnecessary and cruel, and also because coastal communities can earn more money from whale watching. New Zealand, for example, earns $120 million a year from whale watching trips.

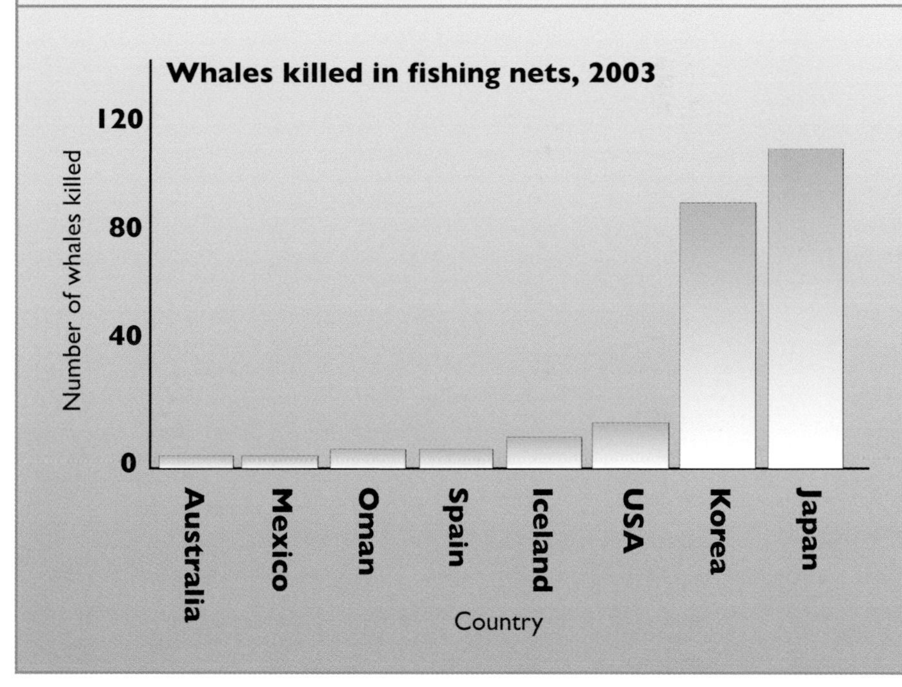

Source: Greenpeace

Coral reefs are where many young fish begin their lives and grow before migrating to deeper waters. It is important not to over-develop and damage such places.

CHAPTER 7

Feed the world

The challenge is to feed adequately a growing global population while protecting the natural systems on which farming depends and allowing everyone a good quality of life.

Nature rules – don't forget it!

Like all animals, humans cannot live without food. Experts predict further developments in farming will be able to support the expected 12 billion people that will inhabit the Earth before the end of this century. To ensure farming is productive and sustainable it must first protect the natural systems on which it depends. These are the soil, other plants and animals, and the various environmental services that ecosystems provide.

Protect soil

Soil is a mixture of minerals, air, moisture, organic matter and living organisms that interact with each other and the air above to form a material in which plants grow. It takes centuries to form, but can be lost in one windstorm or flood. Around 15 per cent of the world's soil is damaged. Soil erosion can be prevented by increasing the organic content of the soil, preventing water from running down slopes, keeping the soil covered with vegetation as much as possible and ploughing it less often. Good farmland is also lost to other uses such as roads, housing, industrial estates and out-of-town shopping centres.

Soil erosion caused by sudden heavy rain has damaged this farmer's field in northern Nigeria. One of the strategies used in this community to try to protect soil and keep it fertile is to use manure from cattle. The farmers have an agreement with Fulani cattle herders: the cattle can graze on the farmland in exchange for their dung, which adds much needed nutrients and improves soil structure by adding organic matter.

These sugar beet plants are wilting due to a lack of rain. Climate change as a result of global warming is causing problems for farmers.

Protect nature

Living things in the soil and the surroundings can help farmers. Living organisms in the soil break down dead vegetation into minerals that the plants can absorb. Leaving space around fields for wild plants encourages insects, birds and other wildlife that can control crop pests without using poisonous chemicals.

It is also important to leave as much natural vegetation as possible. It provides services such as flood control for free. For example, woodlands help to control flooding. Rain hits the trees and then drips to the ground much more slowly. Some evaporates back into the air. The roots of the trees prevent soil from being washed away and the water runs off less quickly and has more time to be absorbed into the ground. Woodlands help control the climate and growing trees absorb some of the excess carbon dioxide produced from burning fossil fuels – one of the causes of global warming.

Global warming

Global warming is a threat to existing farming patterns. Extreme weather conditions, such as hurricanes, tornadoes and storms, can destroy a crop. Changes to the climate may make some areas unsuitable for farming. On the other hand, some areas unsuitable for farming may become more suitable.

Plans for farming in the 21st century must recognise the need to protect the environment, or it will never be sustainable.

Feeding everyone and making farming sustainable will be difficult in the 21st century unless a number of issues are tackled.

Environment

Protecting the environment has to have the highest priority because a damaged environment will be incapable of supplying sufficient food.

Poverty

About 800 million people do not have enough food, most because they are too poor to buy it. Some of the causes of poverty are found in the way food is traded. For example, cocoa farmers in Ghana remain poor because rich countries charge higher tariffs on processed goods, such as chocolate, than on primary goods, such as cocoa beans.

Irrigation helps crops grow, but sprays like these are very wasteful of water, especially when used during a hot day.

Many farmers would be able to improve their farming if they could invest in their farms. However, in many poor countries farmers do not own their land or their homes and so have nothing to borrow money against in order to invest in their farms.

Farm subsidies hurt farmers in developing countries. Europe pays its sugar beet farmers about 1.7 billion euros in subsidy. This encourages overproduction, so Europe also provides export subsidies, which force sugar prices down on the world market. To make matters worse for overseas sugar producers, the EU imposes high import tariffs on most countries wanting to sell their sugar into the EU. This farming system is unfair to poor farmers.

Waste

A lot of food is wasted between harvest and the plate. Fresh food is most vulnerable because it does not keep for long. Refrigeration, freezing and packaging make food last longer. It is also possible to genetically change crops so that fresh foods last longer on the shelf.

Use of resources

Farming needs to reduce its use of energy, chemicals and water if it is to become sustainable. There are already shortages of irrigation water and conflict is likely between countries wanting access to the same water supplies. More efficient irrigation schemes can reduce the amount of water needed, and international agreements can help share out the water resources fairly.

Organic farming may be more sustainable, but not if it uses lots of water and the produce is transported half way around the world before it is eaten.

While 800 million people do not have enough food to eat, elsewhere huge quantities of food are thrown away. Thousands of imperfect bananas have been dumped in this drainage ditch in Costa Rica. This is clearly a massive waste of food.

Eating as if the world really mattered

Everyone is a food consumer and so everyone has an opportunity to change farming. The result of our decisions should be a sustainable and sufficient food supply. Here are some actions to think about. There are no 100 per cent right or wrong actions; every decision made will have some positive and some negative consequences. The important thing is to think about the issues, learn about them and then make a decision that you believe to be right at the time. Later, you may wish to change it. They are not presented in order of priority. That is something for you to decide as well.

- Avoid buying more food than needed.
- Save and eat up leftover food: this reduces food wastage and therefore the need to grow more food.
- Compost food waste: compost can be used to improve the soil.
- Become a vegetarian: eating plants direct (not eating animals that have eaten plants) reduces the loss of energy in the food chain.
- Buy Fair Trade Food: you know the farmers have received a fair price for the produce and will be able to support their families and communities.
- Join an organisation that campaigns for policies you believe in: there are many organisations supporting things such as Fair Trade, changes to food tariffs and subsidies, organic farming and local food production.

The Live 8 concerts in 2005 attempted to encourage political leaders from the world's richest countries to change their policies and make the world a fairer place for all.

Source: FOA statistics division, 2004

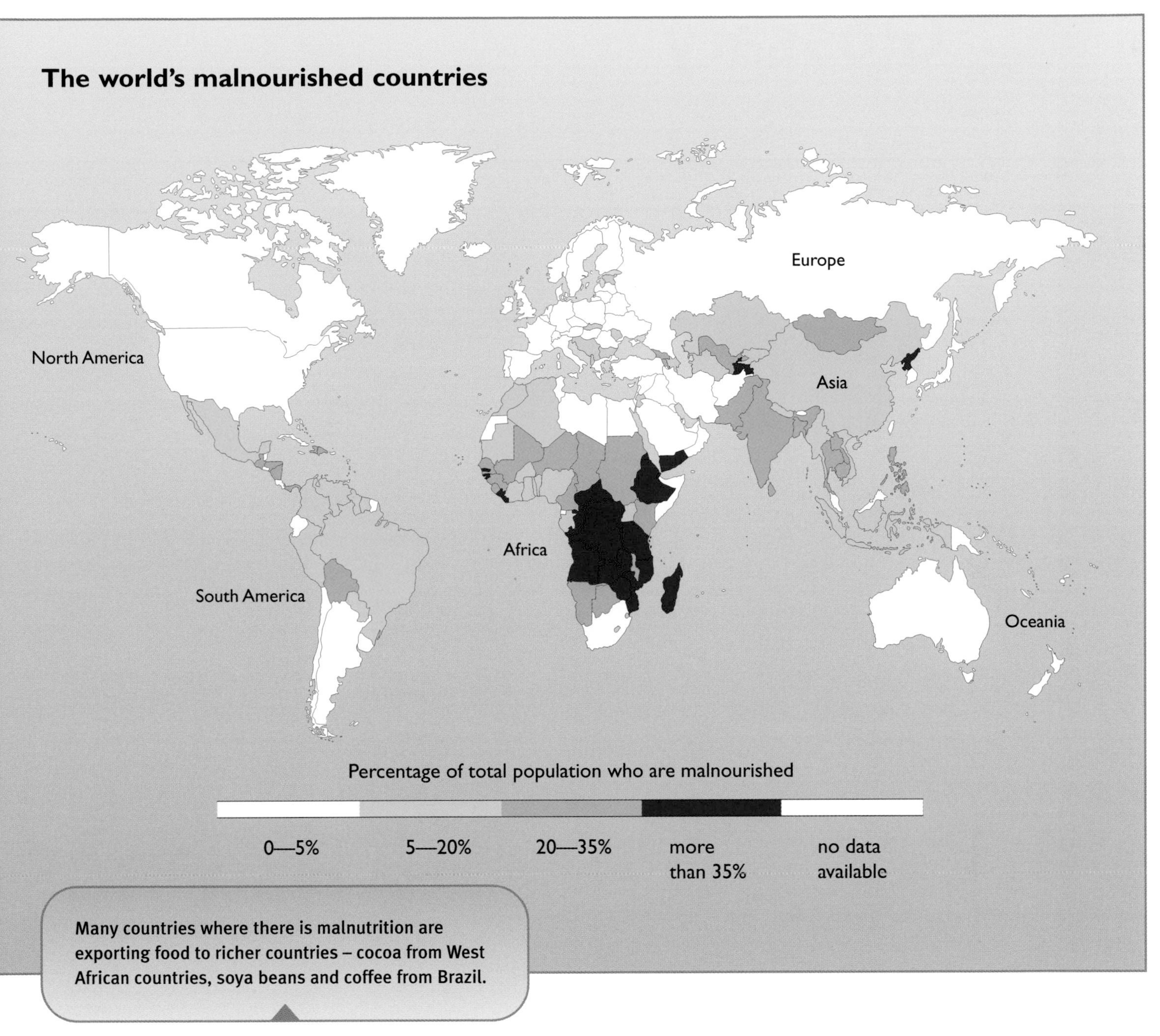

Many countries where there is malnutrition are exporting food to richer countries – cocoa from West African countries, soya beans and coffee from Brazil.

- Grow some of your own food: most of us can cultivate some of our own food, even if it is only in a window box. The more you grow, the less land is needed elsewhere for growing food.
- Buy locally produced food: if food is produced and eaten locally it saves on food miles and therefore fuel, and supports the local community. Farmers' markets only sell local food.
- Buy fish from sustainable fisheries: look for the seal of approval from the Marine Stewardship Council.
- Buy animal products from humanely treated animals: animals should not have to suffer more than necessary for our convenience.
- Discuss your ideas with others: exchanging ideas helps you learn about issues and make more informed decisions.
- Eat a healthy diet: eat fresh foods rather than processed ones and don't overdo the things that are not good for you such as fatty and sugary foods. For a healthy life, it is recommended to eat at least five portions of fresh fruit and vegetables a day.

Glossary

aquaculture farming of fish and other sea life

arable farming farming of plant crops such as wheat, maize or vegetables

cash crop crop grown for sale abroad rather than for food in the area where it is grown

commodity raw material or agricultural crop, such as wheat, which can be bought and sold

deforestation clearing of trees from an area

developed countries richer, industrialised countries of the world including the USA, Australia, Japan and European countries

developing countries poorer countries of the world, such as some African, Asian and South American countries, which are aiming to develop

diversify be more varied; do, or produce, a variety of different things

ecosystem all the plants and animals in an area, along with their environment

fertiliser substance, natural or man-made, that is added to soils to maintain or improve their fertility

fishery fishing ground, or place where fish are caught

food chain series of creatures that are each dependent on the next as a source of food

food miles amount of miles produce has travelled before it reaches the consumer

genetically modified crop crop produced by plants that have had their genetic structure altered to produce effects that are beneficial to humans

global warming gradual increase in the overall temperature of Earth's atmosphere

habitat natural home or environment of a living thing

herbicide chemical used by farmers to control weeds in their fields

infrastructure basic physical and organisational structures, such as buildings, roads, power supply and water supply. Farming needs the right infrastructure in order to be successful.

intensive farming farming that aims to produce large amounts of food from a small area of land. It uses high levels of machinery, chemicals, fertiliser and feed. Livestock kept in intensive conditions are said to be factory farmed.

irrigation supplying water to farmland usually by a system of canals and pipes

malnourished lacking proper nutrition. Malnutrition happens when people do not have enough food to eat, or when they are not eating enough of the right foods.

multinational company large company or business that operates in many countries

omnivore person or animal that has a varied diet, including meat and plants (vegetables)

organic farming farming that does not use any man-made chemicals whether as pesticides, herbicides or fertilisers

pastoralist sheep or cattle farmer

pesticide chemical used by farmers to control insect pests in their fields or on their livestock

photosynthesis process by which plants use the Sun's energy, water and carbon dioxide to form carbohydrates. Oxygen is released in the process.

quota limited quantity of a crop or product that can be harvested, exported or imported. A quota on fish states how many fish can be caught.

soil erosion wearing away of the soil and land by rain, rivers or wind

steppe large area of flat, unforested grassland in south-east Europe or Siberia

sustainable development development that does not cause long-term damage to the environment or deplete natural resources while improving people's quality of life

yield amount of a crop that is produced or harvested

Further information

Contacts

Food and Agriculture Organisation of the United Nations (FAO)
Is helping to build a world without hunger.
http://www.fao.org/

Friends of the Earth
Has national groups in many countries dealing with a range of issues, including sustainable development. Type "Friends of the Earth" into your search engine to find your national or local group.

Greenpeace
Is an international organisation with a presence in 40 countries across Europe, the Americas, Asia and the Pacific. It also has national and local groups providing information on their campaign topics including: Save the oceans, Stop whaling, Say no to genetic engineering, Encourage sustainable trade.
http://www.greenpeace.org/international

The International Federation of Agricultural Producers
Represents over 600 million farm families in 110 national organisations in 75 countries. Farmers from industrialised and developing countries exchange concerns and set common priorities. Its website has information about sustainable farming.
http://www.ifap.org/en/index.html

The International Federation of Organic Agriculture Movements
Is the worldwide umbrella organisation for the organic movement. It provides information about organic farming. http://www.ifoam.org

The Marine Stewardship Council (MSC)
Is an independent non-profit organisation that promotes responsible fishing practices and certifies sustainable fishing. http://www.msc.org

Sustain: The Alliance for Better Food and Farming
Has up-to-date information on all the issues surrounding food and farming in the UK.
http://www.sustainweb.org

The Worldwatch Institute
Is a leading source of information on how we can change to an environmentally sustainable and socially just society.
http://www.worldwatch.org

The World Trade Organisation
Is the only international organisation dealing with the rules of trade between countries. It was established in 1995 and is based in Geneva.
http://www.wto.org

WWF
Has a global marine programme providing information on fishing and its effects.
http://www.panda.org

Government Departments of Agriculture
Provide information on sustainable farming. Go to your government's home page to find out more.

National Sustainable Agricultural Information Service
Is funded by the US Department of Agriculture to provide information and assistance to farmers, educators and others involved in sustainable agriculture.
http://www.attra.org

Books

Earth's Precious Resources: Soil, Ian Graham (Heinemann Library, 2004)

Eyewitness Guides: Food, Laura Buller (Dorling Kindersley, 2005)

Green Files: Climate in Crisis, Steve Parker (Heinemann Library, 2004)

Life Files: Food Matters, Jillian Powell (Evans Brothers, 1998)

Pachamama: Our Earth – Our Future (Evans Brothers, 2002)

Sustainable Human Development: A Young Person's Introduction, Peace Child International (Evans Brothers, 2003)

Index